Why Read Thoreau's *Walden?*

Why Read Thoreau's *Walden?*

Daniel G. Payne

2013
New Street Communications, LLC
Wickford, RI

newstreetcommunications.com

All photos: Renee Johnson. Used by permission.

2013
New Street Communications, LLC
Wickford, Rhode Island
newstreetcommunications.com

To Jim McCord, teacher, mentor, and friend,
and his wife Carol, with gratitude and affection

Contents

From the First Edition:

Thoreau's cabin as drawn by his sister Sophia.

Why Read Thoreau's *Walden*?

1

Thoreau's Declaration of Independence

Early in the spring of 1845, twenty-seven year old Henry Thoreau walked the two miles from his native village of Concord, Massachusetts to Walden Pond, where he intended to build a small cabin in the woods on the northern shore of the pond. He had been given permission to build the cabin there by his friend and mentor Ralph Waldo Emerson, who owned the woodlot; the axe he carried for the job was also borrowed from a friend. "It is difficult to begin without borrowing," wrote Thoreau, "but perhaps it is the most generous course thus to permit your fellow-men to have an interest in your enterprise." By May Thoreau had cleared enough land and hewed enough timber to put up the frame for his house and had carried two cart-loads of stones from the pond to serve as the foundation for the chimney, which he would complete before cold weather set in. After siding and shingling the cabin, Thoreau moved in on July 4, 1845. He claims in *Walden* that beginning his "experiment" on the anniversary of America's Declaration Independence was merely a coincidence, but the thematic emphases of the book suggest otherwise. He lived at Walden for just over two years and the book he wrote about his experience, *Walden, or Life in the Woods* (1854), has become one of the great classics of American literature that has enabled countless readers to "have an interest" in his enterprise.

Like some of the other great works of Anglophone literature such as James Joyce's *Ulysses*, Herman Melville's *Moby-Dick*, and Walt Whitman's *Leaves of Grass*, Henry Thoreau's *Walden* has earned a reputation as a daunting read. There is some justification for this perception; Thoreau is a philosopher of the first order and is not afraid to challenge his readers with ideas and assertions that demand serious thought. In a sense, the book is a Socratic dialogue, with Thoreau at one end of the conversation and the reader at the other. The absence of any sustained narrative thread in *Walden* is also a challenge for many readers, as Thoreau offers us ideas to consider, not a tale for our entertainment—although it should be noted that the book is generously laced with Thoreau's clever wordplay and sly humor. There are a multitude of reasons why *Walden* is one of the undisputed masterpieces of American literature and why, despite the challenges, it is a book well worth reading When I first read the book in my teens, much of the wisdom contained in its pages was beyond my comprehension, and yet, Thoreau's independent outlook, his love of nature, and his epigrammatic wisdom resonated and found purchase with my still inchoate young mind. Many of Thoreau's aphorisms were soon committed to memory and now, decades later, remain there as fresh and vivid as they seemed the first time I found them in the pages of *Walden*:

- "The mass of men lead lives of quiet desperation."

- "Beware of all enterprises that require new clothes, and not rather a new wearer of clothes."

- "A man is rich in proportion to the number of things which he can afford to let alone."

- "We must learn to reawaken and keep ourselves awake, not by mechanical aids, but by an infinite expectation of the dawn, which does not forsake us in our soundest sleep."

- "I went to the woods because I wished to live deliberately, to front only the essential facts of life, and see if I could not learn what it had to teach and not, when I came to die, discover that I had not lived."

- "Our life is frittered away by detail…Simplify, simplify."

- "I learned this, at least, by my experiment; that if one advances confidently in the direction of his dreams, and endeavors to live the life which he has imagined, he will meet with a success unexpected in common hours."

- "If you have built castles in the air, your work need not be lost; that is where they should be. Now put the foundations under them."

- "Why level downward to our dullest perception

always, and praise that as common sense? The commonest sense is the sense of men asleep, which they express by snoring. Sometimes we are inclined to class those who are once-and-a-half witted with the half-witted, because we appreciate only a third of their wit."

- "Why should we be in such a desperate haste to succeed, and in such desperate enterprises? If a man does not keep pace with his companions, perhaps it is because he hears a different drummer. Let him step to the music which he hears, however measured or far away."

- "The light which puts out our eyes is darkness to us. Only that day dawns to which we are awake."

There is also Thoreau's comment on reading that seems particularly apropos when applied to his own work: "Books must be read as deliberately and reservedly as they were written."

Thoreau's family was not wealthy by any means, but they knew the value of a good education, and so they encouraged their son Henry to apply to Harvard College. Although he barely passed the required entrance examination, Thoreau matriculated at Harvard in 1833. Very few young men (and even fewer young women) were fortunate enough to receive a college education in those days, and the financial sacrifice made by Thoreau's family was a hardship rewarded by his graduation (in the middle of his class) in 1837. After Thoreau graduated from Harvard he took a job as a teacher in a Concord school but soon resigned from that position when he was told that he would be required to enforce discipline by corporal punishment. The following year Thoreau opened a private school where he could educate students as he saw fit; a few months later with the school enjoying more success than Thoreau had initially anticipated, his brother John, two years Henry's senior, joined him on the faculty. For a time things went very well for the Thoreau brothers' school, but when John came down with a fatal case of tetanus in January 1841 after cutting himself while shaving, Henry developed a sympathetic case of lockjaw that his family feared would claim him as well. The school closed shortly thereafter, and Thoreau was once again left to his own devices, writing essays and poems, working as a land surveyor, tutoring young students (including Emerson's children), and helping his father in a pencil manufacturing business located in the Thoreau family's boarding house.

Given the literary renown of *Walden,* it may come as a surprise to learn that the writing project that Thoreau first undertook at his cabin on the pond was about a boat trip on the Concord and Merrimack Rivers that he and his brother John had taken in 1839. *A Week on the Concord and Merrimack Rivers* (1849) was Thoreau's first book, and a tribute of sorts to his brother, although John is never mentioned by name in the book, but is referred to only as Thoreau's "companion." *A Week on the Concord and Merrimack Rivers* received mixed reviews; in particular, many reviewers took offense at Thoreau's disparaging remarks about organized religion: "It would be a poor story to be prejudiced against the life of Christ because the book had been edited by Christians," Thoreau writes, but he then goes on to challenge what he saw as the empty religious conventions of many professing Christians. New England's churches, he observed were not truly centers of Christ's teachings, but merely of empty superstition, "so that when one enters a village the church, not only really but from association, is the ugliest looking building in it, because it is the one in which human nature stoops the lowest and is most disgraced." Not surprisingly, such views weren't well-received by the majority of Thoreau's contemporaries and the book sold very poorly. Thoreau's Boston publisher, James Munroe and Company published 1,000 copies of *A Week on the Concord and Merrimack Rivers* but less than three hundred were sold and in 1853 Munroe shipped the remaining seven hundred books to Thoreau, who wryly noted in his journal that he now possessed "a library of nearly nine hundred volumes, over seven hundred of which I wrote myself."

The dismal reception of *A Week on the Concord and Merrimack Rivers* affected Thoreau's work on *Walden,* which he had hoped would be published shortly after his first book came out. Thoreau had already completed a first draft of *Walden* while he was still residing at Walden Pond, but after the disappointment of *A Week* and its effect on his already precarious finances it took another five years and multiple revisions until he—and his new publisher Ticknor and Fields in Boston— felt that the book was ready for publication. As Thoreau scholar Lawrence Buell writes, the delay in publication and subsequent revisions improved the book immensely: "This was trying for Thoreau, but good for posterity. Had *Walden* been published as originally planned, it would have been remembered as a provocative autobiographical reminiscence and an incisive critique of conventional ways of making a living, but not as the intricate and challenging work of close description and knotty philosophical-poetic reflection that it became."

Walden sold better than *A Week on the Concord and Merrimack Rivers* had, but it still did not sell out the initial run of 2,000 copies until 1859, five years after it was published. As was the case with Herman Melville's *Moby-Dick* it would take many years for *Walden* to gain recognition as one of the most important works in American literary history. Thoreau never expected that the book would find a popular audience among the "mass of men" whose minds were primarily turned toward commerce and the necessity of eking out a living, although this was the audience that might well have benefited most from his message. Like his brother John, Thoreau died tragically early, succumbing to the 19th century scourge of tuberculosis in 1862, when he was just forty-four years old.

It would be spurious to deny that *Walden* is a challenging read that not only demands concentration, but also invites you to pause in your reading often enough and long enough to fully consider what is being said. A careless or inattentive reader may well find *Walden* to be inscrutable or simply dull; a fully engaged reader will find that essaying to untangle the "knotty philosophical-poetic" ideas contained in *Walden* is well worth the effort, and by the 20th century *Walden* was finally recognized as one of the great masterpieces of American literature. Succeeding generations have found the lessons contained in *Walden* to be as timely and valuable as they were when Thoreau first wrote the book, embracing Thoreau's ideas on the value of wilderness (and wildness); the benefits of a life led simply rather than succumbing to rampant consumerism and needless complexity; and the cultivation of a sense of mindfulness conducive to spiritual and emotional well-being and growth. *Walden* is also frequently acknowledged as the fountainhead of modern environmentalism, and the place where Henry Thoreau built his cabin near the pond has become sacred space for the hundreds of thousands of readers who have made literary pilgrimages to the place where Thoreau conducted his philosophical experiment in living. In 1872 Bronson Alcott, a friend of Thoreau's (and father of Louisa May Alcott, the author of *Little Women*) brought Mary Newbury Adams, a visiting friend from the Midwest, to the spot where Thoreau's cabin had been. As a contemporary of Thoreau's, Alcott remembered where the site was, but he and Adams lamented that there was no commemorative marker to indicate where the cabin stood, so they each placed a rock on the site as a token of love and respect for Thoreau and his work. The custom lives on to this day, and (despite some efforts in the past by park authorities to discourage the practice) the rock cairn at Walden Pond is a living, growing monument to the impact that Thoreau and his work have had on readers over the past century and a half.

In my first semester as an undergraduate at Union College in the late 1970s, I was fortunate enough to take a course in American literature with Jim McCord, a wonderful teacher and poet, who took our class on a field trip to Concord, Massachusetts to visit Walden Pond and the other literary landmarks of Concord. While time and development had significantly changed the area—the edition of *Walden* he assigned for the course contained an excellent essay by E.B. White that eloquently addressed this issue—the experience was a formative one, even if it took me many years to fully realize how profoundly influential it was. In the intervening years I have re-read *Walden* countless times and have assigned it (or parts of it) numerous times in my courses on American literature.

Each time I come back to the book I find something different, something I never noticed before, often a passage relevant to the perpetually changing circumstances and interests in my own life. To me this is one of the indications of a literary work of surpassing genius—a work that is so reflective and encompassing of life and the world around us that it continues to grow and change, for and with the reader, with every passing season.

Reconstruction of Thoreau's cabin at Walden Pond.

Literary Nationalism & Transcendentalism

On October 22, 1837, a few months after graduating from college and returning to Concord, Thoreau ran into Ralph Waldo Emerson, a fellow resident of Concord and graduate of Harvard. Emerson was then thirty-four years old, a former Unitarian minister who was now making a reputation as a philosopher, writer, lecturer, and one of the young nation's most original thinkers. In 1836 his anonymously published treatise *Nature* had created something of a sensation in the American literary and artistic communities that chafed under the palpable contempt that many critics in Europe had for the work of the nascent arts and letters community of the United States. In a widely circulated article that appeared in the January 1820 edition of the *Edinburgh Review*, critic Sydney Smith wrote, "During the thirty or forty years of their independence, [the Americans] have done absolutely nothing for the Sciences, for the Arts, for Literature, or even for the statesman-like studies of Politics or Political Economy… In the four quarters of the globe, who reads an American book? or goes to an American play? or looks at an American picture or statue?" Fifteen years later in his classic study *Democracy in America* (1835), Alexis de Toqueville—who was alternately laudatory and repelled by what he saw in America during his extensive travels through the states during the early 1830s, wrote:

> *I readily admit that the Americans have no poets...In Europe people talk a great deal about the wilds of America, but the Americans themselves are insensible to the wonders of inanimate nature, and they may be said not to perceive the mighty forests which surround them till they fall beneath the hatchet. Their eyes are fixed upon another sight: the American people views its own march across these wilds,— drying swamps, turning the course of rivers, peopling solitudes, and subduing nature.*

Although de Toqueville's characterization of the American experience was, for the most part, on the mark, even before he had written these words there was a movement afoot in America to remedy this situation. In the visual arts, with Thomas Cole in the vanguard, a loose affiliation of landscape painters including Asher Durand, Thomas Cropsey, and Frederic Church realized that while America might not have the magnificent cathedrals, castles, and two thousand year history of Europe, the untamed mountain ranges of New York and New England, the great rivers, the seemingly limitless prairies, and the primeval forests of America were just as, if not more, magnificent and sublime as anything to be found in Europe. The "wilds of America" became the inspiration for what became known as the Hudson River school of landscape painting, the first great American artistic movement. Likewise, in American literature, writers such as Washington Irving, James Fenimore Cooper, and William Cullen Bryant—often in association with the Hudson River school painters—were also drawing from the American wilderness as inspiration for their fiction and poetry.

It took Ralph Waldo Emerson, however, to take the disparate strains of the new American offerings in art and literature and weave them into a loose set of principles that distinguished the Americans from their European predecessors. The opening lines of *Nature* are often referred to as America's "Intellectual Declaration of Independence," with its clarion call for Americans to free themselves of European traditions and attitudes and go directly to nature to seek revelation and insight:

> *Our age is retrospective. It builds the sepulchres of the fathers. It writes biographies, histories, and criticism. The foregoing generations beheld God and nature face to face; we, through their eyes. Why should not we also enjoy an original relation to the universe? Why should not we have a poetry and philosophy of insight and not of tradition, and a religion by revelation to us, and not the history of theirs? Embosomed for a season in nature, whose floods of life stream around and through us, and invite us by the powers they supply, to action proportioned to nature, why should*

> *we grope among the dry bones of the past, or put the living generation into masquerade out of its faded wardrobe? The sun shines to-day also. There is more wool and flax in the fields. There are new lands, new men, new thoughts. Let us demand our own works and laws and worship.*

In succeeding essays and lectures such as "The American Scholar" (1837), his "Divinity School Address" (1838), and "Self-Reliance" (1841) Emerson built upon his argument in *Nature* and inspired many young Americans to cast aside the bounds of tradition and to go to nature and personal insight as scholars rather than to merely rely on "the mind of the past." So when Thoreau and Emerson met on the streets of Concord, Emerson took a kindly interest in his young neighbor, asking him "What are you doing now?" Although Thoreau undoubtedly mentioned that he was now teaching in Concord and living again with his parents in their boarding house, he certainly realized that Emerson had a larger question in mind—to quote a line from "The Summer Day" by the modern poet Mary Oliver, perhaps the gist of his question was really this: "Tell me, what is it you plan to do/with your one wild and precious life?" Before they parted ways, Emerson (who wrote in one of his essays, "Pay so much honor to the visits of Truth to your mind as to record those thoughts that have shone therein.") advised Thoreau to keep a journal. When he returned home later that day, Thoreau wrote: "'Do you keep a journal?' [Emerson] asked. So I make my first entry today." For the next twenty-five years Thoreau faithfully kept his journal, recording not just his activities and ideas, but creating a remarkable natural history of Concord and its surrounding environs, including a compendium of local plants and animals, precise meteorological information, and minute observations of the seasons. Not only has his journal become a valuable storehouse of information about one of America's foremost writers, but modern scientists have found it to be a useful source in examining the effects of climate change on the northeastern United States.

The Transcendentalist movement in the United States is often seen as an offshoot of European Romanticism, and this linkage provides a convenient starting point for any discussion of what Transcendentalism represents in terms of American intellectual history. Like the Romantics, Transcendentalism was a movement away from traditional religious dogma and toward a spiritual insight arising directly from nature and the individual soul. But while it is fairly easy to identify the spiritual and religious aspects of Transcendentalism as a core belief shared by many of those who identified themselves as Transcendentalists, the movement was comprised of such a disparate, individualistic group of freethinkers that it is rather difficult to come up with an all-encompassing definition of Transcendentalism. As literary scholar Joel Myerson writes, "Defining transcendentalism is a lot like grasping mercury: both are fluid and hard to pin down." Emerson offered a vague definition in his 1842 essay "The Transcendentalist," writing, "What is popularly called Transcendentalism among us is Idealism: Idealism as it appears in 1842." He does go on to say, in a somewhat more helpful vein, that:

> *The Transcendentalist adopts the whole connexion (sic) of spiritual doctrine. He believes in miracle, in the perpetual openness of the human mind to new influx of light and power; he believes in inspiration, and in ecstasy. He wishes that the spiritual principle should be suffered to demonstrate itself to the end, in all possible applications to the state of man, without the admission of anything unspiritual; that is, anything positive, dogmatic, personal. Thus, the spiritual measure of inspiration is the depth of the thought, and never who said it? And so he resists all attempts to palm other rules and measures on the spirit than its own.*

At its heart, therefore, Transcendentalism is essentially a religious phenomenon, but one that was also rooted in the spirit of independence, self-reliance, and nature study. As Emerson would describe in more detail in "The American Scholar," the three great influences on the mind of a young scholar were first and foremost, Nature; second, the mind of the past as conveyed by parents, teachers, and books; and finally, the scholar's own experience. Emerson's teachings struck many young Americans of the Nineteenth- century as a philosophy of spiritual liberation that encouraged them to be independent thinkers questioning all the old teachings and assumptions and discarding whatever seemed to be out of touch with their own soul.

Thoreau was, in many ways, the living embodiment of Emerson's description of the ideal "American Scholar." Emerson praised the study of natural history as being on a spiritual par, or in many ways, superior to— established religions, citing the notion of correspondence developed by the philosopher Emmanuel Swedenborg. The study of nature, he asserted, will reveal that "nature is the opposite of the soul, answering to it part for part. One is seal, and one is print. Its beauty is the beauty of his own mind, Its laws are the laws of his own mind. Nature then becomes the measure of his attainments. So much of nature as he is ignorant of, so much of his own mind does he not yet possess. And, in fine, the ancient precept 'Know thyself,' and the modern precept, 'Study nature,' become at last one maxim." Thoreau took this principle to heart and his studies of natural history, much of which is recorded in his journal, were extraordinarily detailed and insightful. As the great nature writer John Burroughs stated, Emerson himself went to the nature not as a scientist, but to "fetch the word of the wood god to men," and his intellectual descendants such as Thoreau, John Muir, and Burroughs himself would far exceed Emerson in terms of their knowledge of natural history.

Emerson's mentorship was invaluable during Thoreau's youth; the exposure to Emerson's liberating ideas, their long discussions of philosophy, literature, and the soul, and Emerson's encouragement of Thoreau's early literary efforts—including publication in the *Dial*, the leading transcendentalist magazine, which Thoreau also edited for a time—were vitally important to the development of Thoreau as a philosopher and a writer. The relationship was by no means a one-sided one; not only was Thoreau an intellectual equal to Emerson (and many critics believe that he surpassed Emerson in terms of the literary quality of his work), but Thoreau was a skilled craftsman who was often called upon by Emerson to work on various projects at Emerson's home. During Emerson's long absences on lecture tours, Thoreau was often asked by his friend to look after the Emerson family, wife Lydian and the Emerson children, who were immensely fond of him. In the late 1840s the friendship between Emerson and Thoreau cooled noticeably, and part of the reason for this has been attributed to Emerson's decision, while he was away on a long European lecture tour, not to immediately return home when word arrived that his son Edward had become seriously ill. Thoreau saw this decision as evidence of a major character flaw and he never saw Emerson in quite the same reverential way again.

Additionally, the independent-minded Thoreau undoubted chafed under the opinion expressed by some of his contemporaries, such as James Russell Lowell, distinguished writer and the editor of *The Atlantic Monthly*, that Thoreau was simply a pale imitation of the great Emerson. Lowell's personal animus toward Thoreau was motivated in part by his editorial decision to redact a passage from Thoreau's essay on the Maine wilderness, "Chesuncook," that appeared in the June 1, 1858 edition of *The Atlantic Monthly* without telling Thoreau or seeking his assent. In that article Thoreau had written:

> *Is it the lumberman, then, who is the friend and lover of the pine, stands nearest to it, and understands its nature best? Is it the tanner who has barked it, or he who has boxed it for turpentine, whom posterity will fable to have been changed into a pine at last? No! no! it is the poet; he it is who makes the truest use of the pine,—who does not fondle it with an axe, nor tickle it with a saw, nor stroke it with a plane,—who knows whether its heart is false without cutting into it,—who has not bought the stumpage of the township on which it stands. All the pines shudder and heave a sigh when that man steps on the forest floor. No, it is the poet, who loves them as his own shadow in the air, and lets them stand. I have been into the lumber-yard, and the carpenter's shop, and the tannery, and the lampblack factory, and the turpentine clearing; but when at length I saw the tops of the pines waving and reflecting the light at*

a distance high over all the rest of the forest, I realized that the former were not the highest use of the pine. It is not their bones or hide or tallow that I love most. It is the living spirit of the tree, not its spirit of turpentine, with which I sympathize, and which heals my cuts. It is as immortal as I am, and perchance will go to as high a heaven, there to tower above me still.

Apparently Lowell found that latter statement a trifle too pantheistic for his taste and deleted it, which greatly irritated Thoreau. Lowell later took a number of literary potshots at Thoreau's work, but as most of them were written safely after Thoreau's death when the object of his barbs was unable to respond, his carping ultimately damaged Thoreau's reputation less than they did his own.

Regardless of any cool periods in his personal relationship with Emerson, from their first meeting in 1837 until his untimely death in 1862, Thoreau found the ideas and people that comprised the phenomenon of American Transcendentalism compatible with his own beliefs and experiences. In early March of 1853, the secretary of the American Association for the Advancement of Science sent Thoreau a questionnaire on behalf of the association that queried about the branch of science he was most interested in. Thoreau dutifully attempted to answer their queries, but noted in his journal "inasmuch as they do not believe in a science which deals with the higher law…I was obliged to speak to their condition and describe to them that poor part of me which alone they can understand. The fact is I am a mystic, a transcendentalist, and a natural philosopher to boot. Now I think of it, I should have told them at once that I was a transcendentalist. That would have been the shortest way of telling them that they would not understand my explanations."

Why Read Thoreau's *Walden*?

22

A CALL TO AWAKEN

In the epigraph to *Walden*, Thoreau writes, "I do not propose to write an ode to dejection, but to brag as lustily as chanticleer in the morning, standing on his roost, if only to wake my neighbors up." To reinforce the importance of that statement he reiterates it in the chapter "Where I Lived, and What I Lived For." He probably believed that the group most likely to wake up before they settled into a dull routine for the remainder of their lives were the young. "Perhaps these pages are more particularly addressed to poor students," he writes. Like Emerson before him, Thoreau had hopes that the young class of "American Scholars" that Emerson had addressed in his 1837 essay of that title had the potential for a life richer in philosophical and spiritual meaning than those who were already yoked to a farm, a business, a family, and other responsibilities that kept them from making decisions free from financial considerations. "The ancient philosophers," Thoreau writes, "Chinese, Hindoo, Persian, and Greek were a class than which none has been poorer in outward riches, none so rich inward… To be a philosopher is not merely to have subtle thoughts, nor even to found a school, but so to love wisdom as to live according to its dictates, a life of simplicity, magnanimity, and trust. It is to solve some of the problems of life, not only theoretically, but practically."

Thoreau understood that some readers might take his confident assertions in *Walden* as self-congratulatory conceit, an attempt to make his reluctance to settle down and take steady work a virtue. "For more than five years I maintained myself thus solely by the labor of my hands, and I found, that by working about six weeks in a year, I could meet all the expenses of living," is a claim that some of his neighbors might cite as evidence of Thoreau's slothfulness, not a virtue—although in the very next sentence he states that by limiting his wants and his need to work to pay for them he had the whole winter and most of the summer free and clear for study. "In short," he writes, "I am convinced, both by faith and experience, that to maintain one's self on this earth is not a hardship but a pastime, if we will live simply and wisely; as the pursuit of the simpler nations are the sports of the more artificial. It is not necessary that a man should earn his living by the sweat of his brow, unless he sweats easier than I do." Thoreau was unmarried and had no children, and so, with no family to support, no debts, and a talent "to want but little," his situation was quite different from that in which most adults find themselves, so it might be tempting to dismiss his ideas regarding the simple, philosopher's life on those grounds. But as he says in the opening pages of *Walden*, "As to the rest of my readers, they will accept such portions as apply to them. I trust that none will stretch the seams in putting on the coat, for it may do good service to him whom it fits."

There is no doubt, however, that Thoreau's message of being fully awake, of being mindful in one's daily activities, is a necessary and universal one: "That man who does not believe that each day contains an earlier, more sacred, and auroral hour than he has yet profaned, has despaired of life and is pursuing a descending and darkening way." What Thoreau was really doing as he built his house, planted his garden, and hoed his beans was a form of mindfulness meditation, and he proudly proclaims "I grew in those seasons like corn in the night." Developing this sense of mindfulness—to be truly awake to all that life has to offer and not to stumble through each day like a somnambulist—was central to Thoreau's experiment at Walden woods. This is a key tenet in many forms of mindfulness training offered by Zen masters and Christian philosophers alike; if one is truly awake, truly mindful to the miracle of our own lives, then a simple act such as washing the dishes—or hoeing beans— becomes a sacrament. Like many other nature writers, Thoreau believes that there can be a deeply spiritual aspect to country life, tied as it is to the rhythms of the sun and the seasons. As anyone who tends a small garden can attest, there is a profound pleasure to be had in coaxing green things to grow and enjoying the fruits (and vegetables) of your labors in the garden at your dinner table. The hard, physical work of gardening without "aid from horses or cattle, or hired men or boys, or improved implements of husbandry," had additional benefits, according to Thoreau: "I was much slower, and became much more intimate with my beans than usual. But labor of the hands, even when pursued to the verge of drudgery, is perhaps never the worst form of idleness. It has a constant and imperishable moral, and to the scholar it yields a classic result."

It takes sustained effort to train oneself to be fully mindful, and so Thoreau urges his readers to "learn to reawaken and keep ourselves awake not by mechanical aids, but by an infinite expectation of the dawn, which does not forsake us in our soundest sleep." These are inspirational words, but Thoreau confesses that even during his residence at Walden Pond his effort to remain mindful did not always meet with success—after just two weeks at his cabin, he noticed that he had trodden a path from his cabin to the pond that he took so regularly that it was still visible five years after he left Walden Pond. "The millions are awake enough for physical labor;" he writes, "but only one in a million is awake enough for effective intellectual exertion, only one in a hundred millions to a poetic or divine life. To be awake is to be alive. I have never yet met a man who was quite awake. How could I have looked him in the face?"

THOREAU'S SENSE OF PLACE

In "The Divine Soil," as essay that appeared in the April 1908 edition of *The Atlantic Monthly,* the great literary naturalist John Burroughs wrote, "The lesson which life constantly repeats is to 'look under your feet.' You are always nearer to the divine and the true sources of your power than you think. The lure of the distant and the difficult is deceptive. The great opportunity is where you are. Do not despise your own place and hour. Every place is under the stars. Every place is the center of the world." This is a sentiment with which Thoreau would have been in complete accordance.

Henry Thoreau's roots in Concord, Massachusetts went deep, and his connection to place permeates his work. Located about twenty miles west of Boston and founded in 1635, Concord was one of the oldest settlements in New England and there was an extensive historical record of the area that Thoreau often draws from in his work. Probably every schoolchild in America—and certainly every one in Concord—was familiar with the battle of Lexington and Concord in 1775. The skirmish between local militia and British troops at the wooden bridge over the Concord River was the first battle of the American Revolution, and "the shot heard round the world" soon passed into legend. Thoreau's parents were hard-working, upright citizens, but not very prosperous; his father, John Thoreau was a shopkeeper and he and his wife Cynthia Dunbar Thoreau had a small farm where Mrs. Thoreau operated a boarding house to supplement the family's modest income. John Thoreau later set up a business manufacturing pencils; with the help of his son Henry, this provided a steady income for the family. Born on 12 July 1817, Henry (whose birth name was actually David Henry Thoreau; Thoreau himself changed the order of his name after graduating from college), Thoreau was the third of four children: Helen (1812-1849); John Jr. (1815-1842); and Sophia (1819-1886). All of the Thoreau children, like their parents, were apparently interested in natural history and spent a good deal of time exploring the woods and fields of Concord and the surrounding region.

The America that Thoreau knew was a place of tremendous change taking place with breathtaking speed. The Louisiana Purchase of 1803 had doubled the size of the new nation and the movement westward, a burgeoning industrial base, and new technologies such as the railroad and telegraph were changing the face of the continent. Commerce and the accrual of wealth were becoming a secular religion in the United States. The United States were also a place of enormous contradictions and paradoxes, the most troubling being the "peculiar institution" of chattel slavery, a practice that was not only at odds with the growing international abhorrence of slavery but, more fundamentally, was anathema to the democratic principles on which the nation was founded. Furthermore, as Alexis de Toqueville had noted, the Americans were so busy "conquering" the wilderness (as well as its native inhabitants) and relentlessly moving the frontier westward that most barely noticed the magnificent landscape of the continent until it had virtually disappeared. There were only a few observers prior to the American Civil War who called attention to the disappearance of the American wilderness: James Fenimore Cooper in his novel *The Pioneers* (1823); John James Audubon in his *Ornithological Biography* (nine vols.; 1831-1839); and George Catlin, who made the first public appeal for the creation of a system of national parks in 1833. Henry Thoreau was one of these far-sighted observers of the American scene. In the June 1858 edition of *The Atlantic Monthly,* Thoreau published the third and final essay of his series on the forests of Maine (later published as *The Maine Woods* in 1864) that decried the destruction of America's great forests and proposed the establishment of national forest preserves:

> *Why should not we…have our national reserves, where no villages need be destroyed, in which the bear and panther, and some even of the hunter race, may still exist, and not be 'civilized off the face of the earth,' —our forests, not to hold the king's game merely, but to hold and preserve the king himself also, the lord of creation, —not for idle*

sport or food, but for inspiration and our own true recreation? Or shall we, like the villains, grub them all up, poaching on our own national domain?

While Thoreau's reference to humankind as the "lord of creation" was facetious, his proposal for national forest preserves was completely in earnest. In his earlier excursions to Maine, he had observed that the seemingly limitless forests of that state were under relentless assault by loggers and settlers and that Maine might soon become as "bare and commonplace" as Massachusetts, acidly commenting that "We seem to think that the earth must go through the ordeal of sheep-pasturage before it is habitable by man." Much of southern New England had already gone through the "ordeal of sheep pasturage" by the early 1800s. As a student of the local lore and natural history of his native village Thoreau was able to imaginatively recreate the process as it had taken place in Concord and its environs. The advance of civilization and "progress" that was so highly valued by Thoreau's contemporaries was something that he observed with a more critical eye. It was, at best, a mixed blessing that had left in its wake a "tamed and emasculated country" he wrote in his journal.

In 1844 a new railroad line was built that linked Concord with the rest of Massachusetts and ran near Walden Pond. Thoreau's comments in *Walden* about the railroad line that ran so close to his cabin, and about the birth of the industrial age in America generally, reflect his internal conflict about such changes. Thoreau raises questions about how the much vaunted increase in speed and efficiency brought about by the spread of railroads affected human society, writing, "We do not ride on the railroad; it rides upon us. Did you ever think what those sleepers are that underlie the railroad? Each one is a man…. The rails are laid on them, and they are covered with sand, and the cars run smoothly over them. They are sound sleepers, I assure you. And every few years a new lot is laid down and run over; so that, if some have the pleasure of riding on a rail, others have the misfortune to be ridden upon." His opinion of the other great technological advance of the era, the telegraph, was just as withering: "We are in great haste to construct a magnetic telegraph from Maine to Texas; but Maine and Texas, it may be, have nothing important to communicate…We are eager to tunnel under the Atlantic and bring the old world some weeks nearer to the new; but perchance the first news that will leak into the broad, flapping American ear will be that the Princess Adelaide has the whooping cough." There is a price to be paid for such technological innovations, Thoreau cautions, and while relatively few people—in his time or ours—ever stop to consider this price, it can be a steep one. When it comes to "modern improvements," Thoreau writes, "there is an illusion about them; there is not always a positive advance. The devil goes on exacting compound interest to the last for his early share and numerous succeeding investments in them. Our inventions are wont to be pretty toys, which distract our attention from serious things. They are but improved means to an unimproved end."

Walden sunrise.

32

HENRY GOES TO FITCHBURG

Thoreau's warning about our fetish for technological playthings rather than "serious things" is even more relevant today than it was in his own time. In the 1850s most people, at least, knew who their neighbors were, where their food came from, how to produce the basic necessities of life, and so on. Today, none of that can be assumed. While ours is often hailed as the "Age of Information" because our technology has made it so easy to acquire access to a seemingly inexhaustible ocean of information, in many ways that information has become a tsunami that has inundated our lives—overwhelming and sweeping away other, perhaps far more important types of information, as Bill McKibben argues in *The Age of Missing Information* (1989), which compares the type of information accrued from twenty-four hours spent in nature to that accrued from twenty-four hours of programming on what was then the largest cable television system in America.

While the point McKibben makes in *The Age of Missing Information* is certainly still a valid one, when I discuss the book with students in my class in environmental literature, they are quick to observe that in the relatively short time since McKibben wrote his book, things have become even more overwhelming in terms of the barrage of information and information technology available today, thanks to the internet and the digital revolution, among other things. Ours has become an era of specialization where we pay people to perform not only difficult tasks—like surgery, higher education, legal work—but also the most mundane of chores, simply because we no longer have the time, inclination, or ability to do them ourselves. "We are made to exaggerate the importance of what work we do; and yet how much is not done by us!" writes Thoreau, and what was true in this respect in his own time has only increased through the years. If there is one thing that we can learn from *Walden*, it is that the wheel of life will continue to turn without offering ourselves as grist for the post-industrial mill.

Perhaps it is because I was born before the internet and other modern technologies became so much a part of everyday life that it is easier for me to moderate my appetite for modern "conveniences" such as text messaging, twitter, Facebook, and video games, to name just a few that now seem pervasive. Once my class is dismissed, many of the students (if they have not already been surreptitiously "texting" during class) spill out into the quad and immediately begin texting furiously, heads down, all attention focused on a tiny cell phone screen. Our roads and highways, already dangerous enough, have become even more perilous since the spread of cellphones and text messaging. Despite the fact that it is now illegal in most states to text while driving, it is pervasive; I doubt there are many drivers who have not had a near accident with someone whose attention is focused not on the task at hand, but is instead locked in on a tiny cellphone that has his or her gaze directed away from the road. Whenever I notice such a driver, it is hard not to think of Henry Thoreau's warning in *Walden*: "Our inventions are wont to be pretty toys, which distract our attention from serious things."

The glut of electronic information upon which we as a society and as individuals are now gorging ourselves, has had a myriad of unintended consequences. Psychologists have now identified "information overload" as a source of mental neurosis, and as news features on National Public Radio and *The New York Times* in the summer of 2013 reported, the problem has become so widespread and worrisome that a growing number of people are paying large sums of money to attend tech-free camps in an effort to break their addictions to their omnipresent electronic devices. As reported on NPR on July 5, 2013, a company called Digital Detox held its first session of a summer camp for adults called "Camp Grounded" in California; despite a fairly hefty price tag of $350 to submit to a three-day program of technological abstinence, the event soon sold out. The campers surrendered their electronic gadgets in an effort to overcome what many described as a sense of "FOMO—fear of missing out" that had now become pervasive and troubling for many of them— an unintended, but not unforeseen consequence of our technological dependence on "pretty toys" as Thoreau warns in *Walden*. Even worse is the recent proliferation of incidents of "cyber-bullying," some of which have been the proximate cause of suicide by the victims of such attacks. What does it say about a society where our love of technology leads, instead of knowledge and wisdom, to vicious and anonymous attacks on the vulnerable, to a despair and loneliness so acute that death seems preferable?

Thoreau illustrates his point about so-called improvements of modern industrial life by means of a seemingly paradoxical response to a friend's invitation to travel by railroad to the nearby town of Fitchburg to see the country. "I am wiser than that," says Thoreau, "The swiftest traveler is he that goes afoot," and he proposes a competition where his friend will travel the thirty miles by rail (paying the fare of ninety cents) and he will walk. To earn the price of the ticket, Thoreau points out, his friend will need first to earn the price of the train fare, which amounts to a day's wages, while he can immediately begin his journey on foot. I will get there by evening, says Thoreau, having enjoyed the walk and seen the countryside at leisure while his friend would have spent most of the day working and—if he is lucky enough to get a job in season and an early evening departure—perhaps his friend would get there the same night, or perhaps the next day. "And so," he concludes, "if the railroad reached around the world, I think I should keep ahead of you; and as for seeing the country and getting experience of that kind, I should have to cut your acquaintance altogether."

While there is a light tone to Thoreau's little parable about the theoretical journey to Fitchburg, his point bears consideration. As he says about the expense of procuring one's clothing in the first chapter of *Walden*, "the principal object is not that mankind may be well and honestly clad, but unquestionably, that the corporations may be enriched." Rather than enrich the railroad by purchasing a ticket and traveling by rail, better to enrich one's own experience by walking and truly getting a chance to see the country. As is often the case with Thoreau's rhetoric, he makes an emphatic point by presenting an extreme version of his argument; on his journeys to Maine and Cape Cod, to name just two examples, he took the train to get there— and *then* embarked on a long walking tour in each case. He is not suggesting that one should never take the train to cut down on travel time, but that travel, and our lives generally, are about more than simply arriving at our destination in the shortest possible time. Not only is it a message that resonates in a world so obsessed with speed —"it's the journey, not the destination that is important," so to speak— but it is one that even a child can comprehend, as beautifully shown in D.B. Johnson's illustrated book for young readers, *Henry Hikes to Fitchburg*.

Detail of Thoreau statue at Walden.

Lives of Quiet Desperation

The first, and by far the longest, chapter of *Walden* is entitled simply "Economy." This chapter is about far more than simply dollars and cents, although Thoreau does give us a precise accounting of how much it cost to build his cabin and what his expenses and income were during his sojourn at Walden Pond. Just a few pages into the chapter, Thoreau offers his memorably-worded assertion that "the mass of men lead lives of quiet desperation," continuing on to say "From the desperate city you go into the desperate country, and have to console yourself with the bravery of minks and muskrats. A stereotyped but unconscious despair is concealed even under what are called the games and amusements of mankind. There is no play in them, for that comes after work. But it is a characteristic of wisdom not to do desperate things." Thoreau's provocative statement invites the reader to ask (at least) two questions: first, what is it about men's (and women's) lives—in his time as well as in our own—that leads to this sense of quiet desperation? And second, what can we do to avoid this common condition of human life?

Thoreau avidly read many of the classic works of eastern philosophy that were being published for the first time in English translations during his lifetime, and there is no doubt that the ideas expressed in *Walden* are influenced by sources from Buddhist, Taoist, and Confucian sources, among others. Thoreau's diagnosis of the source of the cultural ills that plague us have more than a passing resemblance to the Four Noble Truths identified by the Buddha: First, human life inevitably includes suffering, for the world and our lives are imperfect and impermanent. Second, the origin of our suffering is attachment, our desperate attempt to cling to things—love, life, possessions—that are by their nature impermanent Third, our suffering can be alleviated by ceasing to cling to the impermanent aspects of our lives and developing a sense of enlightened detachment. Fourth, the path to the cessation of suffering is attainable through the Eightfold Path, a form of self-improvement that avoids the extremes of hedonism and asceticism—hence the reference to Buddhism as "the Middle Way."

"Men labor under a mistake," Thoreau writes, and that mistake is in placing value on possessions that will ultimately rob them of the most precious commodity of all: the all too brief time which is allotted to us on earth. Playing on a common colloquialism he says that it is impossible to "kill time" without injuring eternity, and what is perceived as a type of good fortune, inheriting property and possessions, is in reality a terrible burden, "for these are more easily acquired that got rid of. Better if they had been born in the open pasture and suckled by a wolf, that they might have seen with clearer eyes what field they were called to labor in. Who made them serfs of the soil? Why should they eat their sixty acres, when man is condemned to eat only his peck of dirt? Why should they begin digging their graves as soon as they are born?" Even worse than gaining possessions outright is borrowing money to pay for them, working to earn money today to pay for a meal you ate yesterday, as Thoreau says. In his novel *Fight Club,* Chuck Palahniuk makes much the same point when the protagonist, as Tyler Durden, says "the things you own end up owning you. It's only after you lose everything that you're free to do anything." In *Fight Club* Durden's plan is to destroy the financial corporations that issue credit cards, loans, and hold debt so that everyone will start over again at zero. Thoreau believes that we should be wise enough to refuse to accrue that debt in the first place, rejecting the consumer impulse that is still at the core of life in America today. It is disturbing that the American people are now commonly referred to as "consumers" rather than "citizens," and I cannot help but recoil whenever I hear this word used to refer to human beings.

The trend toward consumerism was closely tied to the Industrial Revolution and urbanization. As the Romantic poet William Wordsworth wrote in 1806, "The world is too much with us; late and soon,/ Getting and spending, we lay waste our powers:/ Little we see in Nature that is ours;/ We have given our hearts away, a sordid boon!" The situation has only worsened over the past two centuries, and when it comes to national and international economies there is nothing more important than "growth," at whatever cost. As Edward Abbey wrote a few decades ago, "Growth for the sake of growth is the ideology of the cancer cell." In China today, the central government is forcing people in rural regions to leave their farmlands and move to the cities, because it is believed that this will encourage consumerism and add a few points to China's Gross Domestic Product. The human and ecological cost of this forced migration appears to be considered irrelevant to the overall goal of economic growth. There are those who resist the siren call of consumerism and who resolve to live simply and to challenge governmental and corporate policies that do not consider the true, non-monetary, cost of unbridled growth and development. These are the people for whom Thoreau's words in *Walden* will provide inspiration: "The greater part of what my neighbors call good I believe in my soul to be bad, and if I repent of anything it is very likely to be my good behavior. What demon possessed me that I behaved so well?"

So, how then do we escape from a life of quiet, resigned desperation? If we consider the source of the troubles and anxieties that seem to be an inextricable part of our existence, Thoreau suggests that we will perceive that they arise from the pursuit not of necessities but of the so-called luxuries of life. "It would be some advantage to live a primitive and frontier life, though in the midst of an outward civilization, if only to learn what are the gross necessaries of life and what methods have been taken to obtain them." Thoreau pares down the necessaries of life to four basic categories: clothing, shelter, food, and fuel. Once these have been procured, he says, there is an alternative to then embarking on the wholesale pursuit of "superfluities," and that is for the person "to adventure on life now, his vacation from humbler toil having commenced." In chapter two, "Where I Lived and What I Lived For," Thoreau goes on to delineate what he sought in his experiment at Walden Pond, his "adventure on life," but although he provides his own example in the opening chapter he acknowledges that it might not apply to everyone's situation: "I do not mean to prescribe rule to strong and valiant natures, who will mind their own affairs whether in heaven or hell," he cautions, "but mainly to the mass of men who are discontented, and idly complaining of the hardness of their lot or of the times, when they might improve them." There is a deceptively facetious tone to Thoreau's statement that he used the time that he didn't waste in the pursuit of material things to serve as "self-appointed inspector of snow storms and rain storms…surveyor if not of highways, then of forest paths and all across-lot routes, keeping them open, and ravines bridged and passable at all seasons, where the public heel had testified to their utility." The point is that the time was his own, to spend as he pleased. In short, he writes, "My purpose in going to Walden Pond was not to live cheaply nor to live dearly there, but to transact some private business with the fewest obstacles."

The greater part of Thoreau's chapter on "Economy" contains his remarks on how simple and inexpensive it was during the course of his experiment to provide for the necessaries of life. For the first necessity, clothing, he suggests that much of the labor and money we spend to acquire clothing is simply to satisfy our love of novelty and the desire to keep up with the latest fashions rather than satisfy any real need. Even in thrifty and democratic New England, he says, people are judged by the clothing they wear, "But they who yield such respect, numerous as they are, are so far heathen, and need to have a missionary sent to them." As is often the case with Thoreau, his advice runs contrary to the popular wisdom with which we are all too familiar from countless clichés on the topic: "clothes make the man," "first impressions are lasting impressions," "wear a suit to talk to a suit," and many others including Polonius's advice to his son Laertes in *Hamlet*: "Costly thy habit as thy purse can buy,/But not express'd in fancy; rich, not gaudy;/ For the apparel oft proclaims the man."

So is the common wisdom wrong about the favorable impression that dressing well and appropriately for the occasion has? Probably not— most of us know from our own experience that while our clothing shouldn't be such an important factor in how we are seen by others, that it often does influence their opinion of us. But here is Thoreau, in another of his widely quoted epigrams from *Walden* proclaiming, "beware of all enterprises that require new clothes." By taking the contrarian position, as he so often does, Thoreau gets our attention (if not our immediate concurrence), but by digging a bit deeper, we get to his real point: not only is it more economical to not purchase new clothing indiscriminately, but as he goes on to say, "beware of all enterprises that require new clothes, and not rather a new wearer of clothes. If there is not a new man, how can the new clothes be made to fit… Otherwise we shall be found sailing under false colors, and be inevitably cashiered at last by our own opinion, as well as that of mankind." In other words, the improvement in one's outward appearance should be matched or exceeded by one within.

Of the four necessities of life—clothing, shelter food, and fuel—that Thoreau discusses in his chapter on economy, he readily admits that while there are some societies who do without shelter, the New England climate makes this impractical. However, he writes, "Many a man is harassed to death to pay the rent of a larger and more luxurious box who would not have frozen to death in such a box as this." The box to which he refers is a 6′x 3′ tool box that railroad workers commonly left near the tracks while they were working. Once again, while Thoreau is overstating to make an emphatic point, the gist of his argument is a sound one. Even in Thoreau's day, most people, especially in larger towns and cities, did not own their own homes, but paid a mortgage or rent to provide shelter for their family. Even for those who managed to pay off their mortgage or inherited a farm or house that was not saddled with debt, he says, the owner may not be the richer for it but paradoxically, all the poorer, "for our houses are such unwieldy property that we are often imprisoned rather than housed in them." The recent mortgage debt crisis that left many homeowners "underwater"—owing more on their home mortgage than the house itself was worth—is a painful example of how Thoreau's point still rings true. Once again, Thoreau directs his remarks regarding the provision of shelter for oneself by using specific details that would particularly resonate with students. After giving a precise account of how much it cost to build his cabin ($28.12½), he says that "the student who wishes for a shelter can obtain one for a lifetime at an expense not greater than the rent which he now pays annually." Along the same lines, he describes how he met his own simple requirements for furniture by crafting it himself: "None is so poor that he need sit on a pumpkin. That is shiftlessness. There is plenty such chairs as I like best in the village garrets to be had for taking them away…Thank God, I can sit and I can stand without the aid of a furniture warehouse."

As for the other two necessities of life, food and fuel, part of Thoreau's experiment included growing his own food, consisting of corn, beans, potatoes, and turnips, supplemented by occasionally fishing from the pond. The food items he couldn't, or chose not to, raise himself—things like rice, salt, molasses, and apples—he was able to purchase with the small profit he gained by selling his crops (particularly the beans) that exceeded what he himself used. "I learned from my two years experience," he writes, "that it would cost incredibly little trouble to obtain one's necessary food, even in this latitude, that a man may use as simple a diet as the animals, and yet retain health and strength." As for procuring the fuel that he needed for cooking and to heat his cabin in the winter, wood was abundant near his cabin and by cutting and splitting it himself he learned that it would thereby serve to heat him twice—once when he cut it, and yet again when he burned it—a true economy.

Simplify, Simplify

As anyone who has ever gone on an extended backpacking trip can testify, some of the most important work is done prior to leaving home, when one must decide what to take and what is best left behind. When it comes to the process of selecting what goes in the backpack and what stays at home, I generally divide my decisions into two categories: first, essentials such as food, proper clothing, water, tent, sleeping bag, and other necessary gear; and second, everything else. By the time my pack is filled with the necessary items from the first category, few things from the second category make the cut; a camera, maybe, or a field guide or other book for quiet hours, or a set of binoculars for birding. Over the years—particularly as I have become older and less willing to carry a pack that weighs fifty pounds or more—I have become more discriminating when it comes to selecting essentials (do I really need five pairs of socks?), and positively ruthless when it comes to the second category.

The choices involved in selecting gear for backpacking encapsulates one of the primary themes developed by Thoreau in Walden: the need to pare down the possessions and distractions that needlessly encumber our lives and to concentrate instead on the truly essential things. As Thoreau writes in "Where I Lived, and What I Lived For," the second chapter of *Walden*:

> *I went to the woods because I wished to live deliberately, to front only the essential facts of life, and see if I could not learn what it had to teach, and not, when I came to die, discover that I had not lived. I did not wish to live what was not life, living is so dear; nor did I wish to practice resignation, unless it was quite necessary. I wanted to live deep and suck out all the marrow of life, to live so sturdily and Spartan-like as to put to rout all that was not life, to cut a broad swath and shave close, to drive life into a corner, and reduce it to its lowest terms, and, if it proved to be mean, why then to get the whole and genuine meanness of it, and publish its meanness to the world; or if it were sublime, to know it by experience, and be able to give a true account of it in my next excursion.*

It seems to me that this is the gist of *Walden* in a nutshell, this was the purpose of his experiment—not to play at being a hermit, plant beans, or even to write a book, but to determine what things were essential to living the philosophic, poetic life to which he aspired.

Thoreau claims that "my greatest skill has been to want but little," and if there is a sermon to be found in the pages of *Walden*, as many have claimed, simplicity may well be the keystone of his gospel. "Our life is frittered away by detail," he states, "Simplicity, simplicity, simplicity! I say, let your affairs be as two or three, and not a hundred or a thousand, instead of a million count half a dozen and keep your accounts on your thumbnail." Over the 160 years since the publication of *Walden*, as modern life has become more and more complicated, a growing number of people have realized that more is not necessarily better, and that simplicity has its own virtue. "Why should we live with such hurry and waste of life?" Thoreau queries, "Let us spend one day as deliberately as Nature, and not be thrown off the track by every nutshell and mosquito's wing that falls on the rails." Perhaps all cellphones should have a feature where incoming text messages are announced not by faux trumpets, church bells or the like, but by a sound that conveys their true lack of importance—the sound of an acorn falling on the forest floor, perhaps.

Today the information that floods our lives comes from a plethora of sources: television, newspaper, radio, blogs, e-mails, text messages and much of the "news" they convey amounts to little more than a nutshell or mosquito's wing. In Thoreau's day it was the newspapers that drew his scorn for the emptiness of the current events reported there. "I am sure that I never read any memorable news in a newspaper," he confidently declares, "What news! How much more important to know what that is which was never old!" As an example of the latter he cites the tale of a messenger in China who was sent by his master to inquire of Khoung-tseu, a philosopher living in another province, about the news there. When Khoung-tseu asked in turn about the news regarding the messenger's master he replied, "My master desires to diminish the number of his faults, but he cannot accomplish it." After the messenger left, Khoung-tseu remarked "What a worthy messenger! What a worthy messenger!" When it comes to "the news that stays news," Thoreau would undoubtedly agree with the sentiment that William Carlos Williams expresses in his poem "Asphodel, That Greeny Flower": "My heart rouses/ thinking to bring you news/ of something/ that concerns you/ and concerns many men. Look at/ what passes for the new./ You will not find it there but in/ despised poems./ It is difficult/ to get the news from poems/ yet men die miserably every day/ for lack/ of what is found there./ Hear me out/ for I too am concerned/ and every man/ who wants to die at peace in his bed/ besides."

Walden, springtime.

An American Scholar

In "The American Scholar" (1837), Emerson discusses the three great influences on the mind of the scholar: Nature; the mind of the past, as conveyed by books, teachers, and parents; and then finally, the scholar's own intuition and experience. Thoreau so closely exemplified Emerson's scholar, particularly in his younger years, that it is not surprising that some (such as James Russell Lowell) saw him as a pale imitation of the master and did not realize that in many ways Thoreau had gone well beyond Emerson's teachings and was creating something entirely new, both in terms of his writing and in terms of how he chose to lead his life. Thoreau opens his chapter on "Reading" by stating, "With a little more deliberation in the choice of their pursuits, all men would perhaps become essentially students and observers for certainly their nature and destiny are interesting to all alike." Ideally, all men and women would be students open to nature and the world around them, willing to learn from the great minds of the past, but then confident enough to take that learning and strike out independently on their own journey through life.

As in "Nature," Emerson opens "The American Scholar" with an intellectual declaration of independence: "Perhaps the time is already come, when it ought to be, and will be, something else; when the sluggard intellect of this continent will look from under its iron lids, and fill the postponed expectation of the world with something better than the exertions of mechanical skill. Our day of dependence, our long apprenticeship to the learning of other lands, draws to a close. The millions, that around us are rushing into life, cannot always be fed on the sere remains of foreign harvests. Events, actions arise, that must be sung, that will sing themselves." Thoreau takes Emerson's comments on breaking free from European traditions and takes it a step farther, referring to the philosophy of the East in a call to break away from the tyranny of time itself: "The oldest Egyptian or Hindoo philosopher raised a corner of the veil from the statue of the divinity; and still the trembling robe remains raised, and I gaze upon as fresh a glory as he did, since it was I in him that was then so bold, and it is he in me that now reviews the vision. No dust has settled on that robe; no time has elapsed since that divinity was revealed. That time which we really improve, or which is improvable, is neither past, present, nor future." As one of the twentieth-century heirs to Thoreau, Henry Beston, wrote in his classic work *The Outermost House*, "creation is here and now."

Thoreau's love of reading, of vicariously conversing with the greatest minds of the past through their books, was not confined to the western tradition. Having received a classical education at Harvard, unlike the vast majority of his contemporaries, Thoreau could read Greek and Latin, so perhaps there is a patina of excessive pride in his assertion that the classics should be read in their original language—although most scholars would agree that this would be preferable, for the intervention of a translator between the writer and the reader adds another potential layer of misunderstanding. But although he was not able to read the ancient Hindu and Chinese philosophers in their native language, and had to eagerly await the latest translations, this does not seem to have blunted his enthusiasm for them in the slightest, so long as the books are "read as deliberately and reservedly as they were written."

As a onetime schoolteacher, Thoreau's pithy comments on the state of education in the 1850s are intriguing. "We have a comparatively decent system of common schools, good for infants only," he remarks, but once the basics are learned our educations often cease. "It is time we had uncommon schools," he proclaims, "that we did not leave off our education when we begin to be men and women. It is time that villages were universities, and their elder inhabitants the fellows of universities, with leisure—if they are indeed so well off—to pursue liberal studies the rest of their lives." Whereas in Thoreau's time "adult education" consisted at best of a town's public library and lyceum, the opportunities are far more extensive in the modern information age. There are many "elder inhabitants," who following retirement do indeed "pursue liberal studies the rest of their lives." "How many a man has dated a new era in his life from the reading of a book," Thoreau delightedly exclaims, "The book exists for us perchance which will explain our miracles and reveal new ones. The at present unutterable things we may find somewhere uttered. The same questions that disturb and puzzle and confound us have in their turn occurred to all the wise men; not one has been omitted; and each has answered them, according to his ability, by his words and life."

In Thoreau's time, as in our own, however, there are relatively few who have the ability to read a book as deliberately and reservedly as it was written. "We are under-bred and low-lived and illiterate," Thoreau remarks, "and in this respect I confess I do not make any very broad distinction between the illiterateness of my townsman who cannot read at all, and the illiterateness of him who has learned to read only what is for children and feeble intellects." Today such a statement might well be scorned as elitist by some, but there have been enough references to the United States in the twenty-first century as a "post-literate" society to give cause for concern. Many of my first year students in literature at the state college where I teach have little inkling of how to read for more than the surface meaning of a written work, of how to use the techniques of "close reading" to dig deeper. "It is not all books that are as dull as their readers," writes Thoreau, and when I hear a student complain that a book is "boring," this generally means that a lesson in close reading is in order; not that dull books don't exist (I've struggled through more than a few myself) but far more often the student has not been adequately prepared to read that book. Once they have been taught to see, all kinds of miraculous things appear that would once have gone unnoticed.

Many of the great literary naturalists, including John Muir, John Burroughs, and Henry Beston, Annie Dillard—as well as Thoreau himself—have emphasized the necessity of training oneself to observe, to learn how to see the concrete and details in the world around us as a threshold to understanding. In this, I often draw an analogy between close reading and the study of natural history in my literature classes. In close reading we look for specifics in the work being studied—the repetition of words, phrases, and images; anomalies that stand out because they are different; context; stylistic and grammatical particulars —and use these to attempt to form patterns in the work that reveal meaning and theme. In studying nature we do the same thing. If one knows nothing about the night sky, the stars and planets are simply a random chaos of tiny points of light on a dark background. But if we learn to "read" the night sky, we can identify specific planets and distinctive stars, to identify star clusters that form patterns that ancient observers named as constellations, and even to tell what direction on the compass we are facing or what time of year it is by these patterns. The same principle holds true for other forms of nature study, the search for concrete, specific details that form a pattern that may reveal meaning. This is the motivation that drove Thoreau throughout his life to note his detailed observations of nature in his journal, a passion that grew in import as his life and studies progressed. Thoreau's study of natural history was not scientific study as we understand it now, but grew out of his desire to know a "whole heaven and a whole earth." As he wrote in his journal, "How indispensable to a correct study of Nature is a perception of her true meaning. The fact will one day flower out into a truth. The season will mature and fructify what the understanding had cultivated. Mere accumulators of facts — collectors of materials for the master-workmen— are like those plants growing in dark forests, which put forth only leaves instead of blossoms."

Henry D. Thoreau

SOLITUDE

In "The American Scholar" Emerson states that if the scholar confines his studies to books, "the mind of the past," instead of seeking his own truth through experience, he will not continue to mature as an intellect:

> *Instead of Man Thinking, we have the bookworm... Books are the best of things, well used; abused, among the worst. What is the right use? What is the one end, which all means go to effect? They are for nothing but to inspire. I had better never see a book, than to be warped by its attraction clean out of my own orbit, and made a satellite instead of a system. The one thing in the world, of value, is the active soul... Man Thinking must not be subdued by his instruments. Books are for the scholar's idle times. When he can read God directly, the hour is too precious to be wasted in other men's transcripts of their readings. But when the intervals of darkness come, as come they must, — when the sun is hid, and the stars withdraw their shining, — we repair to the lamps which were kindled by their ray, to guide our steps to the East again, where the dawn is. We hear, that we may speak.*

During his time at Walden Pond, Thoreau did not neglect this aspect of Emerson's strictures. "I did not read books the first summer;" he writes in *Walden*, "I hoed beans." As he writes in a chapter devoted to his bean-field, "I came to love my rows, my beans, though so many more than I wanted." Oddly enough, he seems not to have had much of a taste for beans and often sold or traded them for rice.

Neither Emerson nor Thoreau believed that one had to be a hermit to cultivate a spiritual life. Thoreau has sometimes been criticized for "playing the hermit" when describing his life at Walden Pond when he was living only about two miles from Concord and—as some critics have carped—could walk to his parents' house for dinner and bring a piece of cake or apple pie back to his cabin while it was still warm. This criticism, however, completely misses the point of Thoreau's experiment at Walden Pond, which did not require a complete withdrawal from society, although he does expound at length on the virtue of solitude. In part, Thoreau is himself to blame for this misapprehension, as in his dialogue between the "Hermit" and the "Poet" in the chapter "Brute Neighbors." In that discourse he refers to himself as the hermit—his friend Ellery Channing plays the role of the poet—but this Socratic dialogue contains much that is meant to be read as a humorous, tongue-in-cheek exchange. Thoreau's independence of mind and habit of making emphatically contrarian statements in his work have fed the notion that he was an anti-social misanthrope; as John Burroughs wrote, Thoreau "would rather open his door to a woodchuck than a man" and Henry Beston, another literary descendant of Thoreau, believed that he "had little heart." The historical record suggests quite the opposite; despite his love of solitude and strong independent streak, Thoreau had a wide circle of friends, and was particularly popular with the Emerson children and other young people in Concord who he often took on hikes and huckleberrying parties. As to the assertion of having "little heart," while Thoreau may not have worn his emotions on his sleeve, when Margaret Fuller Ossoli (a Transcendentalist writer and editor) perished with her husband and young child when their ship returning from Italy sank off the shores of Long Island, it was her friend Henry Thoreau who traveled to Fire Island, the great barrier beach of southern Long Island, in an effort to find their bodies and bring them home to Concord for a proper burial.

It should also be kept in mind, particularly in the context of such statements as "I never found the companion that is so companionable as solitude" or "I have a great deal of company in my house; especially in the morning, when nobody calls," that Thoreau had a fairly large family and his mother ran a boarding house; in other words, he was a person who was surrounded by people every day of his life until he went to the woods—by that point he probably craved some solitude! There is also, of course, a vast difference between being solitary and being lonely. One can be lonely in the midst of a city of millions or, like Thoreau, feel perfectly content while alone in nature. He opens the chapter by stating, "This is a delicious evening, when the whole body is one sense, and imbibes delight through every pore. I go and come with a strange liberty in Nature, a part of herself." Like John Muir, who commented that one benefit to being familiar with all the species of trees was that when you were in the woods you were always surrounded by friends, Thoreau feels completely at home in nature because he is himself part of nature: "Shall I not have intelligence with the earth? Am I not partly leaves and vegetable mould myself?"

Thoreau's grave, Concord.

Reading the Book of Nature

In chapters such as "The Ponds" and "Baker Farm," Thoreau's talent for precise, beautiful imagery is clearly evident. In the latter chapter, for example, he describes the extraordinary experience of standing "within the very abutment of a rainbow's arch, which filled the lower stratum of the atmosphere, tinging the grass and leaves around, and dazzling me as if I looked through colored crystal. It was a lake of rainbow light, in which for a short while, I lived like a dolphin. If it had lasted longer it might have tinged my employments and my life." His use of figurative language to embellish his descriptions is also masterful, as in this description of Walden Pond: "A lake is the landscape's most beautiful and expressive feature. It is earth's eye; looking into which the beholder measures the depth of his own nature. The fluviatile trees next the shore are the slender eyelashes which fringe it, and the wooded hills and cliffs around are its overhanging brows."

As the imagist poet William Carlos Williams exhorted, "no ideas but in things," and Thoreau often uses a concrete description of something from nature to serve as a springboard for an abstract idea. Ralph Waldo Emerson, who realized that he had a tendency to rely too much on abstractions in his own writing, appreciated Thoreau's ability to find images from nature to illustrate his ideas. Shortly after Thoreau's death in 1862, Emerson read his friend's remarkable journal and noted in his own "I find the same thought, the same spirit that is in me, but he takes a step beyond, & illustrates by excellent images that which I would have conveyed in a sleepy generality." In one of his last essays, "Walking," Thoreau enunciated a standard for nature writing that beautifully encapsulates his own work:

> *Where is the literature which gives expression to Nature? He would be a poet who could impress the winds and streams into his service, to speak for him; who nailed words to their primitive senses, as farmers drive down stakes in the spring, which the frost has heaved; who derived his words as often as he used them,— transplanted them to his page with earth adhering to their roots; whose words were so true and fresh and natural that they would appear to expand like the buds at the approach of spring, though they lay half-smothered between two musty leaves in a library,— ay, to bloom and bear fruit there, after their kind, annually, for the faithful reader, in sympathy with surrounding nature.*

Of course, like John Burroughs's tersely stated method of turning his studies of natural history into literature —"Truth of seeing and truth of feeling are the main requisite: add truth of style and the thing is done"— the principle and the practice of great nature writing are generally not so easily reconciled.

Thoreau's studies of the natural history of his native Massachusetts were exhaustive and are not only reflected in the pages of *Walden* and his other published works, but in his remarkably detailed journal. He describes the woods, fields, and inhabitants of Concord with fresh eyes, as though he was a visitor from a far away place—which is what he means when he says "I have traveled a good deal in Concord." He observes his native village and its environs with the same alert, inquisitive attention that a scientist on an expedition to a previously unexplored corner of the world would employ. He voraciously read the histories of Massachusetts to gain a sense of what the region was like when European explorers first arrived, and was keenly interested in the American Indians of the region, whom he believed had an understanding of the land that the new arrivals could barely imagine.

Having invested so much time and effort in learning to read the book of nature it is completely understandable that Thoreau had something of a proprietary interest in the state of that book. Thoreau carefully read through many of the early historical documents describing the settlement of New England, and after reading William Wood's *New England's Prospect* (1639) in 1855, just one year after the publication of *Walden*, he compared the catalogue of regional plants and animals in Wood's time with his own and dolefully listed the large number of species that were now rarely found or even completely vanished from the area. The following year he complained in his journal,

> *I take infinite pains to know all the phenomena of the spring, for instance, thinking that I have here the entire poem, and then, to my chagrin, I hear that it is but an imperfect copy that I possess and have read, that my ancestors have torn out many of the first leaves and grandest passages, and mutilated it in many places. I should not like to think that some demigod had come before me and picked out some of the best of the stars. I wish to know an entire heaven and an entire earth. All of the great trees and beasts, fishes and fowl are gone. The streams, perchance, are somewhat shrunk.*

It is sobering to think that this passage was written many years before our own modern era. Biologist and author E.O. Wilson estimated in 1993 that we are now losing something on the order of 30,000 species per year, and many scientists have come to refer to this phenomenon, this stunning loss of biodiversity, as the earth's "Sixth Extinction." To continue with Thoreau's metaphor of ripping pages out of the "book of nature," at this rate we may soon no longer have a book at all, having sadly reduced the natural world to the biodiversity equivalent of crib notes.

In his chapter entitled "The Ponds," Thoreau beautifully describes Walden and some of the other nearby ponds of Concord, places where he confesses to having "spent [his] hours lavishly; nor do I regret," he writes, "that I did not waste more of them in the workshop or the teacher's desk." Just in the few years between leaving his cabin and Walden and revising the manuscript for the book, however, he had noticed a disturbing change in the landscape: "But since I left those shores the woodchoppers have still further laid them waste, and now for many a year there will be no more rambling through the aisles of the wood, with occasional vistas through which you see the water. My Muse may be excused if she is silent henceforth. How can you expect the birds to sing when their groves are cut down?" These groves "were the shrines I visited both summer and winter" he states, and given this spiritual connection with Walden's woods, it comes as no surprise when he takes this sentiment a step further at the conclusion of his chapter on "The Ponds": "Nature has no human inhabitant who appreciates her. The birds with their plumage and their notes are in harmony with the flowers, but what youth or maiden conspires with the luxuriant beauty of Nature? She flourishes most alone, far from the towns where they reside. Talk of heaven! ye disgrace earth."

The Savage and the Civilized

It may seem odd, particularly in a chapter entitled "Higher Laws," to open as Thoreau does here in *Walden*: "As I came home through the woods with my string of fish, trailing my pole, it now being quite dark, I caught a glimpse of a woodchuck stealing across my path, and felt a strange thrill of savage delight, and was strongly tempted to seize and devour him raw; not that I was hungry then, except for that wildness he represented." It must first be acknowledged that the woodchuck, familiar denizen of cultivated fields and vegetable patches, is but a very small portion of wildness by almost any standard. Second, how does devouring this small, rodent-like animal raw, even it just metaphorically, relate to the topic of higher laws or satisfy a desire for wildness?

In considering Thoreau's comments on the civilized and the wild in *Walden* it is helpful to bring into consideration his comments on that topic in one of his late essays, "Walking," published shortly after his death in 1862. The essay opens with a clear statement of purpose: "I wish to speak a word for nature, for absolute Freedom and Wildness, as contrasted with a freedom and Culture merely civil, — to regard man as an inhabitant, or a part and parcel of Nature, rather than a member of society. I wish to make an extreme statement, if so I may make a emphatic one, for there are enough champions of civilization; the minister, and the school-committee, and every one of you will take care of that." As is often the case with Thoreau, it would be easy to misread this passage, and "Walking" as a whole, as a one-sided, full-throated attack on civilization; but what he is really doing is calling for balance. He feels compelled to stake out an extreme position on the virtues of wildness because the case for the other side of the proposition, the value of the "civilized," is already so well established and has so many champions that there is no need to praise its virtues further. From a rhetorical standpoint, Thoreau's advocacy of the wild in "Walking" is akin to the argument that Rachel Carson makes regarding the use of chemical pesticides in *Silent Spring*. Carson never argued (despite what her detractors in the chemical pesticide industry and their political allies claimed) that chemical pesticides should be banned; her argument was that such dangerously toxic substances should only be used with full awareness of potential harmful, and unintended, consequences. Many in the chemical pesticide industry slammed *Silent Spring* as a one-sided attack on pesticides, and accused Carson of intentionally ignoring their utility, but as Carson responded, there were already hundreds of millions of dollars being spent by industry touting the virtues of chemical pesticides, and her book was meant to illuminate a side of the issue that had been conveniently ignored by their proponents.

In "Walking," Thoreau links wildness, freedom, and the West as a unified trinity, writing, "Eastward I go only by force; but westward I go free...I should not lay so much stress on this fact, if I did not believe that something like this is the prevailing tendency of my countrymen. I must walk toward Oregon, and not toward Europe. And that way the nation is moving, and I may say that mankind progress from east to west." Even during the height of the notion of "manifest destiny," there were some, such as Thoreau who saw a darker side to the "conquest" of the American frontier. The United States Congress commissioned an enormous mural painting by Emmanuel Gottlieb Leutze entitled "Westward the Star of Empire Takes Its Way" (1861) glorifying westward expansion to hang in the Capitol Building, but just a few years later, another artist, Andrew Melrose, painted a work that evoked Leutze's painting (Melrose even called his work "Westward the Star of Empire Takes Its Way") but Melrose's painting portrayed an element of tension between the spread of civilization and the destruction of the wilderness. It would not be until the late Nineteenth Century, however, when the American wilderness was all but gone, that historians such as Frederick Jackson Turner in his essay "The Significance of the Frontier in American History" and Theodore Roosevelt in works such as *The*

Winning of the West and "The Strenuous Life" would fret about what the disappearance of the frontier would mean to Americans as individuals and as a nation.

Neither Turner nor Roosevelt cited Thoreau in their works, but "Walking" contains the essence of their arguments; as Thoreau writes:

> *The West of which I speak is but another name for the Wild; and what I have been preparing to say is, that in Wildness is the preservation of the world. Every tree sends its fibres forth in search of the Wild. The cities import it at any price. Men plow and sail for it. From the forest and wilderness come the tonics and barks which brace mankind. Our ancestors were savages. The story of Romulus and Remus being suckled by a wolf is not a meaningless fable. The founders of every state which has risen to eminence, have drawn their nourishment and vigor from a similar wild source. It is because the children of the empire were not suckled by the wolf that they were conquered and displaced by the children of the northern forests who were.*

This beneficial mix of wildness and civilization, says Thoreau, once again anticipating Turner and Roosevelt, applies to the individual as well as the nation: "I would not have every man nor every part of a man cultivated, any more than I would have very acre of earth cultivated; part will be tillage, but the greater part will be meadow and forest, not only serving an immediate use, but preparing a mould against a distant future, by the annual decay of the vegetation which it supports."

Thoreau's sense of social history was undoubtedly linked to his studies of natural history, where he had noticed that it was the ecotone (as modern ecologists would later term it), the border between different ecosystems, that tends to be richest in its diversity of species. As for himself, he says in his essay, "I feel, that with regard to Nature, I live a sort of border life, on the confines of a world, into which I make occasional and transient forays only, and my patriotism and allegiance to the state into whose territories I seem to retreat are those of a moss-trooper." In *Walden,* referring to the cultivation of his bean-field he makes a similar point, saying "Mine was, as it were, the connecting link between wild and cultivated fields; as some states are civilized, and others half-civilized, and others savage or barbarous, so my field was, though not in a sense, a half-cultivated field."

So, to return to Thoreau's "Higher Laws" and his statement about "devouring the woodchuck for that wildness he represented," Thoreau is once again making an extreme, hyperbolic statement so as to make an emphatic point and here that point is once again about the value of wildness. "Once or twice," he writes in *Walden,* "while I lived at the pond, I found myself ranging the woods, like a half-starved hound, with a strange abandonment, seeking some kind of venison which I might devour, and no morsel could have been too savage for me. The wildest scenes had become unaccountably familiar. I found in myself, and still find, an instinct toward a higher, or, as it is named, spiritual life, as do most men, and another toward a primitive, rank and savage one, and I reverence them both." During the two years he spent at Walden Pond, Thoreau sought to satisfy his yearning for wildness with the first of his three trips to the deep woods of Maine, finding atop Mount Katahdin during that initial trip that the sublime, untrammeled wilderness could prove—at least initially—to be an overwhelming experience:

> *Here not even the surface had been scarred by man, but it was a specimen of what God saw fit to make this world. What is it to be admitted to a museum, to see a myriad of particular things, compared with being shown some star's surface, some hard matter in its home! I stand in awe of my body, this matter to which I am bound has become so strange to me. I fear not spirits, ghosts, of which I am one, — that my body might, — but I fear bodies, I tremble to meet them. What is this Titan that has possession of me? Talk of mysteries! — Think of our life in nature, — daily to be shown matter, to come in contact with it, — rocks, trees, wind on our cheeks! The* solid *earth! the* actual *world! the* common sense! Contact! Contact! Who *are we?* Where *are we?*

Thoreau's initial experience with truly wild, sublime nature may have been a disorienting experience as this passage indicates, but it apparently did not last for long. By the time of his second trip to Maine in 1853 he had no such apprehension about entering what he had initially referred to as the "grim, untrodden wilderness," writing instead that by the time he reached Bangor, the last settled area on the way north to the Maine woods, "I began to be exhilarated by the sight of the wild fir and the spruce tops, and those other primitive evergreens peering through the mist in the horizon. It was like the sight and odor of cake to a schoolboy."

Thoreau maintained a vegetarian diet for much of his adult life, stating in "Higher Laws" that "Is it not a reproach that man is a carnivorous animal? True, he can and does live, in a great measure, by preying on other animals; but this is a miserable way,— as any one who will go to snaring rabbits, or slaughtering lambs, may learn,— and he will be regarded as a benefactor of his race who shall teach man to confine himself to a more innocent and wholesome diet. I have no doubt it is a part of the destiny of the human race, in its gradual improvement, to leave off eating animals as surely as the savage tribes have left off eating each other when they came in contact with the more civilized." When Thoreau went to the Maine woods, however, part of his motivation was to gain more firsthand information about the way in which the Indians there lived a life in nature, and he was particularly interested in observing a moose hunt. When he finally did have an opportunity to witness such a hunt on his third trip to Maine, he was very nearly sickened by the killing and skinning of the moose, comparing the hunt to going out by night and shooting one of your neighbor's cows—in other words, there was nothing particularly ennobling about the activity. He admits in *Walden* that it is hunting and fishing that first sends boys to the woods, and this in itself is good, but he qualifies this by stating, "no human being, past the thoughtless age of boyhood, will wantonly murder any creature, which holds its life by the same tenure that he does. The hare in its extremity cries like a child. I warn you, mothers, that my sympathies do not always make the usual phil-*anthropic* distinctions."

Walden Woods, winter.

House Warming

By the time the north wind began to cool Walden Pond during Thoreau's first autumn months at his cabin, he had already begun his preparations for cold weather, completing work on his fireplace, plastering the walls, and chopping wood for his winter fires. These tasks, as well as the seasonal transition from summer to autumn are described in the chapter entitled "House-Warming." In Thoreau's day wood was not only the building material of choice in most regions of the country, but also the primary source of fuel; and the seemingly limitless forests of New England were fast disappearing as the demand for wood increased yearly. "It is remarkable what a value is still put upon wood even in this age and this new country," writes Thoreau, "a value more permanent and universal than that of gold…In this town the price of wood rises almost steadily, and the only question is, how much higher it is to be this year than it was the last." The deforestation of New England and the eastern seaboard had already been proceeding for some two centuries, and whereas Francis Higginson could write in *New England's Plantation* (1630) that the vast forests of the region provided "good living for those that love good fires," just over a century later the woodlands near the growing cities of the northeast had been so depleted, and the price of firewood had risen so high, that in Philadelphia a public-minded citizen named Benjamin Franklin invented a new and more energy-efficient stove that he called the Pennsylvania Fireplace (not, as is commonly thought, the eponymous "Franklin Stove," although that was what it commonly came to be known) and declined to take out a patent on the invention because he believed that conserving fuel was a public good that ought not enrich one man.

Wood was abundant at Walden Pond, however, and Thoreau considered cutting and splitting wood to be fully in keeping with his philosopher's soul: "Every man looks at his wood-pile with a kind of affection. I love to have mine before my window, and the more chips the better to remind me of my pleasing work." The room in my house where I write has a fireplace that I frequently use during the cold months, and I can attest to the truth of Thoreau's statement regarding the physical pleasure of splitting wood and then stepping back to admire a steadily growing woodpile. I would only add that there are few activities more conducive to dispelling the irritations of the modern workplace than the primeval activity of splitting wood. The direct connection to providing the fuel Thoreau used to heat his cabin in the winter, and the satisfaction derived from providing that fuel is something that relatively few of us today experience. Our fuel (number two fuel oil or natural gas) is delivered by pipeline or delivery truck, and other than paying the bill for the fuel and its delivery our primary link to heating our home or apartment is to adjust the thermostat. While it would be contrarian to the extreme to suggest that this has not been a positive development in many ways, it is striking how many writers who have depended on a hearth and fire speak of it in intimate, even affectionate ways. In *The Outermost House* (1928) Henry Beston says of the fireplace in his isolated dune shack on the great beach of Cape Cod, "my fire was more than a source of heat—it was an elemental presence, a household god, and a friend." Likewise, in his short story "I and My Chimney," Herman Melville dwells at length on the peculiar (and strongly symbolic) link between the narrator and his fireplace. Thoreau was just as fond of his fireplace and describes it in human terms: "I sometimes left a good fire when I went to take a walk in a winter afternoon; and when I returned three or four hours afterward, it would still be still alive and glowing. My house was not empty though I was gone. It was as if I had left a cheerful housekeeper behind. It was I and Fire that lived there; and commonly my housekeeper proved trustworthy."

Of course, one of the dangers of relying so heavily on wood as building material and fuel was the risk of house fires and Thoreau's "cheerful housekeeper" was not always so trustworthy. He goes on to describe a near mishap that occurred one day while he was splitting wood and chanced to look in the window of his cabin: "I looked and saw that a spark had caught my bed, and I went in and extinguished it when it had burned a place as big as my hand." In the next chapter of the book "Former Inhabitants; and Winter Visitors," Thoreau describes a barn fire that took place near Concord village a few years earlier. The cry of "Fire!" in colonial and early American communities was a dreaded sound and called forth a burst of activity on the part of all neighbors to sally forth to fight the blaze. The alarm went up, "It's Baker's barn!" recalls Thoreau and then the town sprang to action, with the members of the ad hoc fire department shouting "Concord to the rescue!" Once they got to the site of the blaze, however, they discovered that the barn was beyond saving, so they finally "retreated without doing any mischief."

There is one significant fire in Concord's recent past that Thoreau does not describe in *Walden*, perhaps as it was one that he himself had a hand in and that still caused him embarrassment to recall. In the spring of 1844—an unusually dry year—Thoreau and a friend, Edward Sherman Hoar, went fishing at Walden Pond. They were in the process of preparing their catch for lunch when their campfire, probably due to a sudden gust of wind, spread to a stand of dry grass and then moved quickly toward the surrounding woods. Thoreau and Hoar tried to stop the fire, but by the time it reached the trees they realized it was too large for them to extinguish by their efforts alone, so

Hoar set off for Concord in their boat while Thoreau dashed through the woods ahead of the blaze to find help. By the time assistance arrived from Concord, the fire was raging out of control, and Thoreau, exhausted from his mad dash for help, was lying on a nearby hill. To the eyes of his townspeople charging to the woods to extinguish the blaze before it reached the town, it probably looked as if Thoreau was simply lounging and observing the fire for which he was in large measure responsible. It took over a full day of frenzied work to halt the spread of the fire, and some of his biographers have asserted that for years thereafter some of Thoreau's townspeople blamed him not only for the fire—which was accidentally, if rather carelessly started—but for insufficient ardor in helping to put it out. It is interesting to surmise that one of Thoreau's late writings, "The Succession of Forest Trees," an essay about restoring deforested regions, was in part inspired by the sight of three hundred blackened acres of Walden's forest that he saw regularly and for which bore a large measure of responsibility.

It is just as likely, however, that Thoreau's ideas on forest regeneration were not simply an outgrowth of his personal experience with the fire at Walden woods, but had more to do with the larger issue of deforestation in New England during the eighteenth and nineteenth centuries. There are times in *Walden*, such as when Thoreau speaks of the "boundless chestnut woods of

Lincoln," a nearby town, that it is difficult not to feel the pang of loss that he did when comparing his New England to the primordial paradise that William Wood described in the mid seventeenth-century. But while there have been and continue to be remarkable changes in the American landscape since the advent of European colonization, there have also been some changes over the past century that may well have favorably impressed Thoreau. For example, wild creatures such as deer, bear, and beaver that had been virtually hunted and trapped out of existence in much of the Northeastern states in the mid 1800s have now returned in large numbers. The movement away from rural life and to urban and suburban centers over the same period has—along with farsighted state and federal efforts to preserve wild areas— has changed the landscape in many places. Vermont, for example, is now a verdant and heavily forested state, but two centuries ago most of the primeval forests of Vermont had been felled, and about ninety percent of the state had been deforested in just the short amount of time since the Puritans landed at Plymouth Rock in 1620.

The notion that *more* land in many parts of the northeast is now forested than was the case in Thoreau's day seems counterintuitive to many people, as I learned during a backpacking trip in the Green Mountains of Vermont with two friends from suburban New York several years ago. As we trekked through the mountainous region, one of my friends paused frequently along the way to curiously eye the old stonewalls that traced their way through the dense woods. At long last he was unable to restrain his incredulity and asked me "Are *all* Vermonters as crazy as the ones who lived here?" When I asked why he thought that was the case, he pointed to a nearby stonewall that snaked into the mountains before disappearing in the underbrush, and replied "why on earth would anyone build stone walls in the middle of a forest?" The notion that this mountainous, lushly forested region of Vermont had once gone through Thoreau's "ordeal of sheep pasturage" nearly two centuries earlier, before being protected as a National Forest and permitted to return to a reforested state seemed almost inexplicable to a person far more familiar with an American landscape that was continually subjected to deforestation, not the opposite.

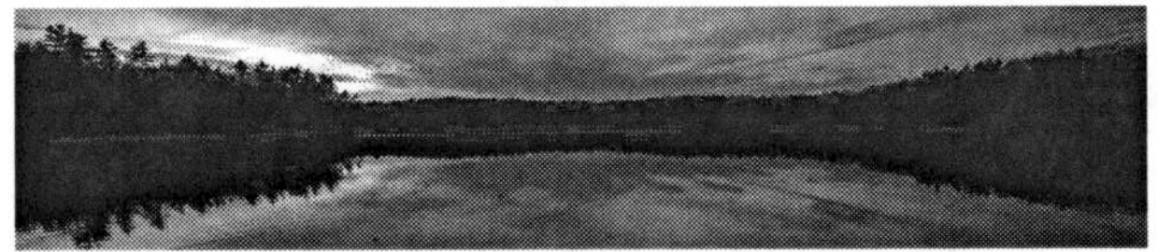

Walden, dusk in winter.

The Seasons at Walden Pond

As with many of the nature writers who followed him, Thoreau structures *Walden* around the passage of the seasons; the structure is often a loose one, and, as he tells us, he compresses the experience of his two years into one for the sake of simplicity. His winter chapters—"Former Inhabitants; and Winter Visitors," "Winter Animals," and "The Pond in Winter"— comprise the longest section of the book with the exception of the opening chapter, which reflects both the length of New England winters and the fact that the cold northern months provided Thoreau with ample time for reflection and writing.

This is not to say that Thoreau neglected his outdoor activities and long walks during the winter. In fact, the freezing over of the pond in winter provided Thoreau, an experienced surveyor, with an opportunity to carefully survey the pond and to plumb its depths to dispel the local myth that it was "bottomless." After his survey, Thoreau was able to "assure my readers that Walden has a reasonably tight bottom at a not unreasonable, though at an unusual, depth" of one hundred and two feet at its deepest spot. He was sufficiently proud of his survey of the pond that he included it in the book as *Walden*'s sole illustration. During the winter of 1846-47 about a hundred men descended on Walden Pond for the ice harvest, which went on for sixteen days, leading Thoreau to boast "Thus it appears, that the sweltering inhabitants of Charleston and New Orleans, of Madras and Bombay and Calcutta, drink at my well."

Thoreau's chapters on the seasons are full of detailed observations, but there is generally no narrative to enliven them, so it is most rewarding to read them at the same contemplative pace that Thoreau advocates when it comes to observing them directly: "One attraction in coming to the woods to live was that I should have leisure and opportunity to see the spring come in." For many years Thoreau kept track of the arrival of spring in his journal, detailing such vernal events as the breaking of the ice on Concord's ponds and river, the arrival of warm weather bird species, the first budding of each variety of tree and flower. "Every incident connected with the breaking up of the rivers and ponds and the settling of the weather is particularly interesting to us who live in a climate of so great extremes," he writes in *Walden*, and in recent years climatologists have used Thoreau's journal as a resource to understanding climate change.

There is a curiously appropriate aspect to Thoreau's new usefulness to modern studies on climate change. Thoreau was born in 1817, just one year after the "Year Without a Summer" in which a temporary climate shift was instigated by a series of events culminating with the spectacular 1815 eruption of Mount Tambora in present day Indonesia. New England was one of the regions in the Northern Hemisphere that suffered far lower than normal temperatures the following year, with spring planting delayed in many places by significant snowstorms coming as late as June and early frosts coming in August. As a result, there were widespread crop failures and famine in parts of the United States, Canada, and Northern Europe. It is small wonder, therefore, that the notion of climate change did not seem so far-fetched to Thoreau, who observes in *Walden* that we need not "trouble ourselves to speculate how the human race may be at last destroyed. It would be easy to cut their threads any time with a little sharper blast from the north. We go on dating from Cold Fridays and Great Snows; but a little colder Friday, or greater snow, would put a period to man's existence on the globe."

Walden, summer.

More Lives to Live

Thoreau left his cabin on Walden Pond on 6 September 1847, declaring, "I left the woods for as good a reason as I went there. Perhaps it seemed to me that I had several more lives to live, and could not spare any more time for that one. It is remarkable how easily and insensibly we fall into a particular route, and make a beaten track for ourselves. I had not lived there a week before my feet wore a path from my door to the pond-side; and though it is five or six years since I trod it, It is still quite distinct." While Thoreau's iconoclasm is sometimes chastised as intellectual arrogance, here is a profound statement of humility; an important aspect of his experiment at Walden Pond was cultivating a sense of mindfulness, to strive to be fully awake to life's possibilities, and in this passage he freely confesses how "easily and insensibly" he fell into a routine despite the fact that he was determined not to do so. Developing mindfulness, as any student of Zen Buddhism, meditation, or yoga understands, is not the work of days, weeks, or months, but is instead a practice refined over years of persistent effort. If Thoreau did not achieve perfect consciousness in his two-year stay at Walden Pond, it was a remarkable beginning, full of profound insight and realizations about the natural world and his own, human nature: "Be a Columbus to whole new continents and worlds within you, opening new channels, not of trade, but of thought...Explore thyself."

In the concluding chapter, Thoreau characterizes the result of his two years at Walden Pond in eloquent terms:

> *I learned this, at least by my experiment; that if one advances confidently in the direction of his dreams, and endeavors to live the life which he has imagined, he will meet with a success unexpected in common hours. He will put some things behind, will pass an invisible boundary; new, universal, and more liberal laws will begin to establish themselves around and within him; or the old laws will be expanded, and interpreted in his favor in a more liberal sense, and he will live with the license of a higher order of beings. In proportion as he simplifies his life, the laws of the universe will appear less complex, and solitude will not be solitude, nor poverty poverty, nor weakness weakness. If you have built castles in the air, your work need not be lost; that is where they should be. Now put the foundations under them.*

Not everyone is suited to, or even aspires to, the philosopher's life that Thoreau prized so highly. Indeed, as he well knew, many of his neighbors saw him as something of an eccentric, and he scoffed at the premium that people placed on "common sense": "Why level downward to our dullest perception always, and praise that as common sense? The commonest sense is the sense of men asleep, which they express by snoring."

In American colleges and universities today there is an ongoing discourse about the plight of higher education generally, and the usefulness of the arts and humanities in particular. The primary goal of many students—and given the increasing debt load of recent graduates, it is an understandable concern—is to find a lucrative job after graduation and to begin to pay down their student loans, beginning a process that continues the rest of their lives—borrowing money to buy a car, taking out a mortgage to own (at least, to partially own) a home, and then, perhaps to borrow money to pay for their own children's college education. From the moment they matriculate, many college students have a career goal, and the matter of actually gaining an education is subsumed by the vocational goal—and more and more college administrators now seem to envision the role of their colleges and universities less as educational institutions than as vocational preparatory schools. Perhaps this is inevitable, given the tendency our society has to assess worth in strictly monetary terms, even with things that can't truly be valued on simply a monetary basis, such as environmental protection, education, and affordable health care. *Walden* reminds us that this is not an exclusively modern phenomenon, that it has long been an issue in American society. "Why should we be in such a desperate haste to succeed," Thoreau queries, "and in such desperate enterprises? If a man does not keep pace with his companions, perhaps it is because he hears a different drummer. Let him step to the music which he hears, however measured or far away. It is not important that he should mature as soon as an apple-tree or an oak. Shall he turn his spring into summer?"

In the conclusion to *Walden*, Thoreau includes a Hindu parable about an artist from the city of Kouroo "who was disposed to strive for perfection." Having decided to carve a staff for his next project he travels to the forest and begins a search for the right piece of wood. By the time he finds the right wood, all of his friends have passed away, but the artist did not grow older by a moment: "His singleness of purpose and resolution, and his elevated piety, endowed him, without his knowledge, with perennial youth. As he made no compromise with Time, Time kept out of his way, and only sighed at a distance because he could not overcome him." By the time the artist had completed his work, cities and dynasties had passed away, and he saw that the elapse of time was an illusion, "and that no more time had elapsed than is required for a single scintillation from the brain of Brahma to fall on and inflame the tinder of a mortal brain. The material is pure, and his art was pure; how could the result be other than wonderful?" While the story of the artist of Kouroo has the opaque quality of a zen koan, its relevance to the philosophy of living that Thoreau has propounded in *Walden* is really quite direct. If one "advances confidently in the direction of one's dreams," and tunes out the din of "our restless, nervous, bustling Nineteenth Century" (or Twenty-First Century, for that matter), our true purpose in life—our "morning work" as Thoreau calls it—will become apparent. While there is, perhaps, a mystical quality to such a statement, ask any artist, musician, writer, or athlete what happens to the passage of time when they are "in the zone."

The closing passage of *Walden* is open-ended, in keeping with the nature of any search for enlightenment and consistent with Thoreau's desire not to teach philosophy, but to live the life of a philosopher. "The life in us is like water in the river," writes Thoreau, "It may rise this year higher than man has ever known it, and flood the parched uplands; even this may be the eventful year, which will drown out all our muskrats. It was not always dry land where we dwell…I do not say that John or Jonathan will realize all this; but such is the character of that morrow which mere lapse of time can never make to dawn. The light which puts out our eyes is darkness to us. Only that day dawns to which we are awake. There is more day to dawn. The sun is but a morning star." The spiritual and intellectual journey that Thoreau describes in *Walden,* and which we embark upon with him as we read his words, is a lifelong one that begins by waking up and

CPSIA information can be obtained
at www.ICGtesting.com
Printed in the USA
LVOW10s1549020217
523022LV00011B/1123/P